BRITAIN IN PICTURES

THE BRITISH PEOPLE IN PICTURES

THE LABOUR PARTY

By courtesy of the Rt. Hon. Clement R. Attlee, the Master of University College, Oxford, and the Artist

THE RT. HON. CLEMENT R. ATTLEE
Oil painting by Oswald Birley, 1947

THE LABOUR PARTY

WILLIAM GLENVIL HALL

WITH
4 PLATES IN COLOUR
AND
22 ILLUSTRATIONS IN
BLACK & WHITE

COLLINS · 14 ST. JAMES'S PLACE · LONDON
MCMXLIX

PRODUCED BY
ADPRINT LIMITED LONDON

PRINTED IN GREAT BRITAIN BY
CLARKE & SHERWELL LTD NORTHAMPTON
ON MELLOTEX BOOK PAPER MADE BY
TULLIS RUSSELL & CO LTD MARKINCH SCOTLAND

JOHN BURNS, 1858-1943

LIST OF ILLUSTRATIONS

PLATES IN COLOUR

BLACK AND WHITE ILLUSTRATIONS

The Editor is most grateful to all those who have so kindly helped in the selection of illustrations, especially to officials of the various public Museums, Libraries and Galleries, and to all others who have generously allowed pictures and MSS. to be reproduced

INTRODUCTION

THE Labour Party was formed at a conference of trade unionists and socialists held in February 1900. Not everyone present on that occasion agreed with the decision to establish it. Some who were there already sat in Parliament as Liberal-Labour Members and not unnaturally wanted this happy state of affairs to continue. John Burns, M.P. for Battersea, disliked the notion of trying to segregate politically the workers in this way. He was, he said bitterly, "getting tired of working-class boots, working-class trains, working-class houses and working-class margarine." Others were against the proposal because they believed the attempt to be a waste of time and energy. As they saw it, the Liberal and Tory Parties were firmly established: no third party could succeed without superseding one of them—a possibility too remote to be taken seriously. The newspapers shared this view. They did not trouble to report the proceedings.

This was not by any means the first attempt to get such an organisation going. Efforts had been made before but they had come to nothing. The vast social and economic problems resulting from the Industrial Revolution had made the century then ending a period of unexampled industrial change and of intense political unrest in which the working classes, from the time of the Chartist and Owenite agitations, had shared. It was however only slowly and as socialism began to gain ground among them that a majority of the organised workers arrived at the belief that their hope of escape from poverty and insecurity lay in the creation of a party of their own.

The Labour Party has been since 1918 a socialist party. It is this fact which marks it off and is the real justification for its right to exist. To its supporters politics is a solemn crusade against social and economic injustices. They believe that only by a drastic alteration in the basis of society can the evils that face a modern State be permanently eliminated. It is this deep and abiding faith which has made countless thousands, unmentioned by name in this narrative, give their time, their money, their comfort, and often their health, to the Movement. Without their devotion it is certain that the Party would never have survived.

The Labour Party is and always has been a democratic Party. It has never flirted with the temptation to advocate physical force as a short cut to power. Throughout, it has relied on persuasion by argument to win support. This, without question, has been a steadying influence in British politics during the last twenty years. For it is not without significance that while the workers in some other countries have fallen an easy prey to totalitarian teaching—either of the Right or of the Left—totalitarianism has made little headway in this country. This has not been due to chance.

Compared with some modern political movements in Europe the rise and growth of the Labour Party has been slow. It took several generations of effort to get itself established and another forty-five years to achieve power. Its influence nevertheless on the legislation of the past forty years has been profound. Since its inception there has been an immense improvement in the lives of ordinary men and women. In 1900 there were no Old Age or Widows' Pensions, no Health or Unemployment Insurance, no Industrial Injuries Compensation or holidays with pay. The social services, as this generation knows them, did not exist. Bumble and the Poor Law reigned supreme. To-day, gone, we hope for ever, are the times when a Ben Tillett could be sent down the mine at the age of eight; a Keir Hardie become a baker's boy and the sole support of his family at the age of six; the mother of a Will Crooks be told by a Chairman of the Guardians that it was high time the boy (then aged eight and off every morning before five to help a milkman for sixpence a week) was "earning his own living."

The workers to-day are better fed, better clothed, better housed, better educated, more secure and live a freer and more leisured existence than did their predecessors fifty years ago. These improved standards are now universally accepted but they have had to be fought for. In the struggles to achieve them, the Labour Movement—political and industrial—has played an overwhelming part.

EARLY REFORMERS

"CIVILISATION," said Tom Paine, "has operated in two ways, to make one part of society more affluent and the other part more wretched than could have been the lot of either in a natural state."

Paine wrote these words before the Industrial Revolution had done its worst. Had he lived another thirty years he would have seen this gap between rich and poor become wider—the degradation of the masses greatly increased, the wealth of the possessing classes enormously extended. By 1840 the productive capacity of the new machines had brought power and prosperity to the manufacturers but only toil, disease and misery to the workers. Men, women and children worked excessively long hours in the factories and in the mines for miserably low wages and spent what scanty free time they were allowed in grimy slums devoid of sunlight and sanitation. A Royal Commission in 1842 found that in some cotton mills children of five worked from fourteen to eighteen hours a day and that others of the same tender age slaved equally long hours in the mines.

Francis Place, 1771-1854
Detail from an oil painting by Samuel Drummond, 1833

Although many employers were genuinely concerned at the havoc they were creating they believed it to be the inescapable consequence of industrial greatness. They were upheld in this opinion by the economic teaching of the day, which most of them accepted without question. They shared with Malthus the fear that without the checks of early death from disease and malnutrition population would quickly outrun food supplies; agreed with Ricardo that enlightened self-interest was not incompatible with the moral law; and out-Adamed Adam Smith in their belief that the more each sought riches for himself the more prosperous the state became since, when all was said and done, the state was nothing more than the sum total of the individuals composing it. The best Government, so they believed, was the one that interfered least.

Fortunately, the workers did not accept the inevitability of their lot with the same cheerful contentment as did their masters. They were however impotent. In the early decades of last century trade unionism was weak, local in character and largely confined to the skilled crafts. The great majority of the workers were poor, uneducated and unorganised and completely at the mercy of their employers who, with the Government to back them and with the excesses of the French Revolution still vivid in their minds, put down with rigorous harshness every effort, however legitimate, to improve conditions.

Luckily, though religion was at a low ebb, humanity in England was not quite dead. There were still some men and women outside the ranks of the toilers who viewed the prevailing doctrines with horror and refused to believe that nothing could be done to help the victims of the system. Although some of these reformers were aristocrats, like Lord Shaftesbury, and some, like Francis Place, successful shopkeepers, they were in the main drawn from the middle classes. John Stuart Mill and Jeremy Bentham were philosopher sons of professional men; Robert Owen and Richard Oastler members in their own right of the new industrial plutocracy.

Shaftesbury is mainly remembered for his efforts to limit the hours and improve conditions for women and children in the factories and for his work to secure better treatment for chimney-boys. To Place we owe the setting-up in 1823 of the Select Committee which recommended the abolition of the Combination Laws. It is true that, being neither a Member of Parliament nor a gentleman, he was not even allowed in the room when the Committee was debating the matter, but with Joseph Hume, who was certainly the former, to present the evidence he had collected, he accomplished his purpose. From then on, in theory at any rate, working men have enjoyed the right to establish their own trade unions.

It is however Robert Owen more than any other individual of that period to whom the modern Labour Movement is indebted. Born in Newtown, Montgomeryshire, in 1771, the son of a saddler and ironmonger, he left home at the age of ten and died in 1858 at the age of eighty-seven. Becoming a rich and successful mill-owner in his early thirties and having learned what he called his great principle—that character is made by circumstance—he filled the remainder of his long life with a succession of social experiments beginning with those he instituted for his workpeople at New Lanark. Sir Leslie Stephen describes him as one of those intolerable bores who are the salt of the earth and there is no doubt that many of his contemporaries found him trying. Most however endured him with good-humoured tolerance, though some, like William Cobbett, treated him with contemptuous ridicule whilst others, like Queen Victoria's father, found him useful as a convenient person from whom to borrow a trifle when funds were low. His schemes unfortunately ended in failure but they excited enormous interest among reformers at the time and, above all, stimulated the working classes to revolt against their lot. The modern Labour Movement remembers him with affection as a pioneer of both the Co-operative Movement and nineteenth-century trade unionism. The

Beginnings of an Event in History—The Tolpuddle Martyrs
Oil painting by Gilbert Spencer, 1946

English word "socialism" came into use to describe the social system he preached.

There was an outburst of activity among trade societies following the repeal of the Combination Laws and many new branches were formed. These had no roots however and most of them did not weather the depression of the late eighteen-twenties. In 1830 the National Association for the Protection of Labour was established, quickly reached a membership of 100,000, but was dead in 1832. Owen's Grand National Consolidated Trades Union, born two years later, enrolled half a million members in a few weeks but also failed to survive. It was in an attempt to establish a union under the inspiration of this second organisation that Loveless and his friends in Tolpuddle met disaster.

Not until, as we shall presently see, the middle of the century and under men of a different stamp, did trade unionism begin to take root and it was later still that socialism, owing little positive to Owenite theories, began to make headway. Nor, except as a lesson in what to avoid, did Owenite propaganda do much to foster the growth of Co-operation.

THE CHARTISTS

OWEN'S Grand National Consolidated Trades Union was born before its time and would have collapsed in any event. Its death was however hastened by the rise of Chartism.

It is customary to trace the rise of the Labour Party to the agitation for the Charter though, truth to tell, the connection is not quite so direct as some suppose. The link however exists, though Radicalism was the immediate gainer and can therefore claim a more immediate relationship. The Chartist Movement is nevertheless a notable landmark in British working class history. It was the first political mass movement of the workers largely led by men of their own class, its aim being to mitigate, by the acquisition of the vote followed by direct Parliamentary action, the social and economic evils resulting from the Industrial Revolution.

Prior to the Reform Act of 1832, out of which Chartism grew, political power in Great Britain resided with the great Whig and Tory families. Whatever their size, counties returned two members elected by the freeholders, whilst local custom alone governed the franchise in the boroughs. Seats were openly bought and sold. Thirty-five constituencies with hardly any voters sent seventy-five members to the House; forty-six with less than fifty electors sent ninety, whilst in others eighty-four male voters returned one hundred and fifty-seven members. The Act of 1832 altered all this. The rotten boroughs disappeared. Birmingham, Manchester, Leeds and other large centres received representation for the first time. Most revolutionary of all, power passed at a bound from the landed aristocracy to the new plutocratic middle classes.

The Reform Act was a bitter disappointment to the masses. They had shared in the struggle for it and, in fact, it had been their energy and violence which had carried the Bill. Yet, when the cheering was over and the triumph had died down, the only tangible result for all their efforts, so far as they could see, was a new Poor Law Act which they found detestable.

The People's Charter demanded universal manhood suffrage; voting by ballot; annual Parliaments; the abolition of a property qualification; and payment of Members. A sixth demand called for equal electoral districts—a change not now considered mathematically feasible. First published in 1838, the chief architects of the Charter were William Lovett and Francis Place. Lovett, upright and self-respecting, was the product of the Mechanics' Institutes, a follower of Robert Owen and an early pioneer of Co-operative shops. Though united on its terms the leaders were sharply divided as to means. There were those, Henry Hetherington and Henry Vincent among them, who believed with Lovett that success should be achieved by persuasion and reasoned argument, whilst others followed Feargus O'Connor, J. R. Stephens and G. J. Harney, whose inflammatory speeches and incitements to force at the great torchlight gatherings held

ROBERT OWEN, 1771-1858
Detail from an oil painting by W. H. Brooke, 1834

up and down the country curdled the blood of all old ladies, in and out of the Government.

Three National Petitions were presented to Parliament, the first, in 1839, by Thomas Attwood, M.P. for Birmingham, whose own particular cure for the ills of mankind was currency reform, not universal suffrage; and the last, in 1848, by Feargus O'Connor himself who made a woeful mess of it, alienating support with every word he uttered. He mustered no more than seventeen followers in the lobby. And, when the Committee appointed to examine the Petition later reported that it contained, not the 5,700,000 signatures grandiloquently claimed by him, but less than 2,000,000, many of which were fictitious, the end had come. Though Chartism failed the effort was not lost. The agitation established, and established firmly, in the minds of the masses a belief in the vote as a thing to be desired and in Parliament as an institution to be valued and used.

As Chartism collapsed, working-class leaders turned once more to trade unionism as a means of alleviating the condition of the workers. Trade unionism revived, but trade unionism of a new kind.

The new leaders were far removed in temperament and outlook from the wild and truculent spirits who had troubled the more sober Chartists. Cautious, self-reliant, self-educated, thrifty and tenacious, they were exactly the men the new organisations needed if these bodies were to be given a chance to survive. The new unions were defensive not militant, constitutional not revolutionary, national not local in scope, and highly selective in that they catered only for the men within a particular craft. The Amalgamated Society of Engineers was the first of them to be established and was followed, ten years later, by the Amalgamated Society of Carpenters and Joiners. Their main feature, as was that of similar organisations which came after, was that they provided, for a relatively high contribution, Friendly Society benefits in addition to the normal benefits of a trade union.

The Corn Laws had by this time been repealed. Free Trade had triumphed. Politically the leaders of the new unions belonged to the Radical wing of Liberalism which, guided by John Stuart Mill, was in the ascendant. They had however little inclination to mix their politics with their trade union activities. To them politics was one thing, trade unionism another. Occasionally someone had the temerity to suggest that the two went very well together. Indeed, in 1857, a half-hearted attempt was made to run George Jacob Holyoake the Co-operator in the Tower Hamlets, but nothing came of this.

THE FIRST CO-OPERATIVE SHOP OPENED IN ROCHDALE IN 1844

The Co-operative Movement had by this time begun to spread. In 1844 twenty-eight poor flannel-weavers in Rochdale, having saved their pennies and opened their own shop, had pointed the way along which success could be achieved. Beginning with groceries and with a stock-in-trade so small that a nearby storekeeper declared contemptuously that he could get the lot of it into a barrow, they went on to provide first meat and then clothing. In sixteen years their tiny capital of £28 had expanded to £120,000 and in addition they had established out of profits a reading-room, a library and a Turkish bath for their members and their members' families. The secret of their success lay in the realisation that earlier experiments had begun at the wrong end. They avoided this mistake by forming a society of *consumers* not producers. Later on the Co-operative Movement was to go into production for itself on an enormous scale but the Rochdale Pioneers were undoubtedly right when they decided to sell at current prices, crediting to each member at periodic intervals his share of the surplus based on his actual purchases. The Movement to-day is a vast trading organisation employing many millions of capital and many thousands of people. It now has twenty-three representatives in the House of Commons who sit and vote as members of the Labour Party. One of its leaders, A. V. Alexander, was First Lord of the Admiralty in the Labour Government of 1929-31 and he also held this Office from 1940, when the National Administration was formed, until it broke up. He returned to the Admiralty again after the General Election of 1945 and remained there until the autumn of 1946 when he became Minister of Defence. Another of its leaders, Alfred Barnes, became Minister of Transport when Labour took office in 1945 and, more recently, Lord Morrison, who had sat for many years as Co-operative Member for North Tottenham before being elevated to the House of Lords, was made Parliamentary Secretary to the Ministry of Works.

George Odger (in Silk Hat)
First Labour Candidate to go to the Poll, 1870

The London Working Men's Union came into existence in 1866 to help in the agitation for an extension of the franchise and to promote working class candidatures for Parliament, but, lacking both money and machinery, it did not function in the General Election of 1868. Three working men did go to the poll however—George Howell, W. R. Cremer and E. O. Greening—but all three fought as Liberals and all failed to get elected.

The first Labour man actually to go to the poll in opposition to both Liberal and

Tory candidates was George Odger, who fought Southwark at a by-election in 1870. Son of a Cornish miner, by trade a maker of ladies' shoes, and a considerable orator, he wielded an enormous influence over London crowds. The Reform Act of 1867 had extended the vote to many working men and this undoubtedly improved his chances. Nevertheless, remembering the date, the result was remarkable. The figures were: Beresford (Tory) 4,686; Odger (Labour) 4,382; Waterlow (Liberal) 2,867. Some accounts describe Odger as fighting as a Radical Working Man but F. W. Soutter who was his election agent affirms in his *Recollections of a Labour Pioneer* that Odger stood as a Labour candidate and was the first to do so. Odger's candidature was promoted by the Labour Representation League, a body then recently formed by trade unionists with the assistance of middle class sympathisers. Its object was "to secure the return to Parliament of qualified working men, persons who by character and ability command the confidence of their class."

Meanwhile the trade unions had begun (1868) to hold a regular annual Congress. Congress however held aloof from the Southwark contest. Nor, although it should have been stimulated to action by that result, did it make any effort either to use the League or to set up an organisation of its own to promote candidatures adequately backed with money. It did however the following year set up a Parliamentary Committee (now the General Council of the T.U.C.) for the purpose, among others, of lobbying Members of Parliament in support of legislation likely to be of benefit to the workers.

The setting-up of the Parliamentary Committee is an event of some significance. Unlike Congress, which only met for a few days each year, the Parliamentary Committee was available all the year round. Its creation is an indication that the organised workers were beginning to feel the need for machinery of some kind to enable direct pressure to be exerted in Parliament, though events were to prove beyond doubt that this cap-in-hand method of approach was both futile and undignified. Congress however took a long time to learn this lesson for even thirteen years later it voted down a proposal to set up a special fund to finance "organised working men" who stood at local and national elections and passed instead an innocuous resolution in favour of the payment of Members of Parliament and the election expenses of candidates. Payment of Members was of course one of the six points of the Charter, of which the only demand met up to then had been voting by ballot. The Ballot Act had been passed in 1872.

Still, some progress was being made. In the General Election of 1874, fired by Odger's gallant fight, the Labour Representation League scored its first successes. Thomas Burt was returned for Morpeth and Alexander MacDonald for Stafford. Both were miners' nominees. At the General Election of 1880 they were joined by Henry Broadhurst who had, as a

H. M. Hyndman, 1842-1921
Bust by Edward H. Lacey

stonemason, helped to rebuild the Palace of Westminster and was afterwards to become Under-Secretary of State for the Home Department.

Although these men stood as working men candidates they were not Labour or Socialist as now understood. They might describe themselves as Radicals but they supported the Liberal Party. Their election finds a place in this narrative because of the evidence it affords of the urge by organised Labour to seek direct representation by its own class and because it was from this growing Liberal-Labour group (which during the eighteen-eighties came to number eleven) that eventually the present Parliamentary Labour Party sprang.

For some reason, in spite of these successes, the Labour Representation League faded away, its place being taken by another organisation brought into existence in 1886 by the Trades Union Congress itself as a sub-committee to act in conjunction with its own Parliamentary Committee. The new body did not remain either a sub-committee or attached to the Parliamentary Committee for very long. It broke away and became an independent organisation known as the Labour Electoral Association, openly allied to the Liberal Party.

SOCIALISM TAKES THE FIELD

TO the onlooker at that time the stage appeared set for the permanent alliance, even the integration, of the direct representatives of Labour with the Liberal Party in the House. This view was illusory. Startling social theories were in the air. A fresh militancy was arising in the unions. More aggressive leaders were entering the lists, challenging the Gladstonian gospel and saying bluntly that another and completely independent party was essential if the masses were ever to obtain justice.

In 1881 the Democratic (afterwards the Social Democratic) Federation had been founded by H. M. Hyndman, a burly, bearded, silk-hatted and frock-coated figure permanently embittered, so his enemies (and they were many) asserted, because his father had left most of his fortune for the building of churches. Hyndman had come under the influence, and had accepted the teaching, of Karl Marx, an individual of great erudition and beaver-like assiduity. Though safely tucked away these many years in Highgate Cemetery his works have unfortunately lived after him and now cast their gigantic shadow over the minds of countless people then unborn. The S.D.F. published a pamphlet, *Socialism Made Plain*, the aim of which was to show that private ownership of the means of production, exchange and distribution was the cause of poverty, and followed up this broadside by the weekly issue of *Justice*, a periodical preaching the same doctrine. William Morris, poet and craftsman, was for a time, until he broke away and formed the Socialist League, a distinguished member of the organisation. The Federation was thus the first of the socialist societies to arise in this country. Its basis was however uncompromisingly Marxian, a creed which has never appealed strongly to the British people.

It was followed, in 1883, by the Fabian Society. Composed overwhelmingly of middle and upper class intellectuals, the Fabian Society sought to influence the public—particularly representatives on local and national authorities—by lectures and the issue of pamphlets. These publications gave socialists for the first time up-to-date facts about social conditions and provided them, as in *Fabian Essays* (brilliantly written by a brilliant team which included Bernard Shaw and Sidney Webb), with a reasoned basis, economic and ethical, for their beliefs. Beyond this the Society did not attempt to go. Fabian Groups were established in various centres but the Society made no attempt to become a mass movement or itself to promote candidatures.

This latter work was undertaken by the Independent Labour Party, a non-Marxian organisation formed under the inspiration of James Keir Hardie at Bradford in 1893. Keir Hardie had been the delegate from a tiny Ayrshire Miners' Union to the 1887 Trades Union Congress where he had aroused the enmity of the bulk of those present by asserting the need

By courtesy of the Glasgow Corporation Art Gallery

RAMSAY MACDONALD ADDRESSING THE FIRST LABOUR GOVERNMENT, 1924

Oil painting by Sir John Lavery

for a political party independent of Liberals and Tories. The following year he translated his belief into action by contesting a by-election in Mid-Lanark. He polled only 712 votes but the episode was the turning-point in his career. From then onwards he devoted himself wholeheartedly to the cause of independence. As a first step the Scottish Labour Party was founded with Hardie as its Secretary.

Whilst these events were taking place in the north, the workers were on the move further south where there was much industrial unrest. The unrest reached a climax in 1889 when the London dockers struck for "a tanner an hour." The strike, led by Ben Tillett, Tom Mann and John Burns, lasted four weeks and ended in a complete victory for the men. The dispute brought the shocking conditions under which the casual workers laboured vividly before the public and, right from the start, the men and their families received support from all sections of the community. A Relief Fund was opened to which all classes, at home and overseas, contributed. It is certain that, just though their claim was, without such aid the men would have been driven back to work by starvation for there was little or no strike-pay in those days. This victory had wide repercussions. Will Thorne (afterwards Labour Member for Plaistow for many years) with Ben Tillett had meanwhile been trying to organise the London gas workers, then working a twelve-hours day, and had met with some success. The triumph of the dockers gave a fillip to these efforts and also led to the formation of other unions. It was now obvious that trade unionism could be extended to the unskilled and to the casual worker.

Interest in social and economic problems had been greatly quickened in the years immediately preceding these events by the lectures of Henry George and the publication of his book *Progress and Poverty* which, Alfred Russel Wallace asserted, was undoubtedly the most remarkable and important book of the century. Henry George, a tiny man with a large head, had been many things in his time—pedlar, tramp, compositor, shop-assistant, farm worker, waiter, inspector of gas meters and free-lance journalist. He was, too, an orator of the first rank. His lecture tours in Great Britain were great triumphs. He was an anti-socialist. His panacea was the Single Tax. Yet, so mysterious are the ways of providence, no reformer of that period did more than he to turn men's minds to socialism or to confirm socialist thinkers in their faith. Bernard Shaw as a young man haunting meetings for practice in voice production heard him and according to Frank Harris "was switched off from Victorian agnosticism and on to economic communism with a flash and a crash." H. G. Wells says in his *Autobiography* that he could not recall having thought about socialism until he read *Progress and Poverty* which, he says, "became a fermenting influence in my mind." Ramsay MacDonald read the book as a young man in Lossiemouth and went through the same experience. "It led men," he wrote later, "to discuss the problem of poverty not as the result of personal shortcomings but as an aspect of a certain form of social organisation."

The formation of the Scottish Labour Party had not passed unnoticed south of the Border. Similar independent Labour organisations began to spring up in many places. The first of these was the Labour Union formed in Bradford in 1890. A few months later enthusiasts in the Colne Valley area of the West Riding set up a similar body which has existed without a break from that day to this and is now known as the Colne Valley Divisional Labour Party. Hardie's objective in establishing the Independent Labour Party was to unite these local groups into one national organisation. He and his friends needed such a body. He was by this time a Member of Parliament, having won West Ham the previous year. John Burns, one of the leaders of the dock strike, had also been successful in the same election. Thirteen other working-men candidates had likewise been returned, but all of these were either in the Liberal or Irish Nationalist Parties and refused to co-operate with Hardie in the House.

The I.L.P. attracted adherents. Its outstanding personalities became well known and were in constant demand as speakers. Unnumbered propaganda gatherings were held—in small back streets, in market squares, in large halls and in tiny rooms. Day after day, unceasingly, the work went on, particularly at week-ends when, without complaint, and as a matter of course, Keir Hardie, Ramsay MacDonald, Philip Snowden, J. R. Clynes, Bruce Glasier and his wife, Margaret Bondfield, Mary MacArthur, Ethel Snowden and many others still affectionately remembered, spent long, tedious hours travelling to and from meetings in all parts of the country. Robert Blatchford, though a poor speaker, was a tremendous asset. His weekly paper *The Clarion* was widely read and cheap reprints of his books, *Merrie England*, *Britain for the British*, and *God and My Neighbour*, sold in their thousands and made countless converts to socialism.

BIRTH OF THE LABOUR PARTY

THE rise of the British Socialist Movement, the successful efforts to extend trade unionism beyond the crafts to the unskilled and casual workers and the growth of feeling in favour of independent Parliamentary representation inevitably had their influence on the Trades Union Congress.

All attempts however to commit Congress to socialism or even to swing it behind the move for independence were frustrated year by year until 1899 when a resolution (carefully prepared by Ramsay MacDonald in the offices of the *Labour Leader*) completely changed the situation. Moved by James Holmes of the Amalgamated Society of Railway Servants

'The Labour Leader,' 1895
Title-page of the paper edited by Keir Hardie

and supported by Margaret Bondfield, later to become the first woman to sit in a British Cabinet, this called on Congress to convene a special conference to devise ways and means for securing the return of an increased number of Labour Members to the next Parliament. It was passed by 534,000 votes to 434,000, in spite of the opposition of Thomas Ashton,

Secretary of the Cotton Spinners, who said that "not one trade unionist in ten thousand would give it a moment's notice" and that "trade unionism would come to grief if it were turned into a political party."

This Conference, momentous as we now realise it to have been, met at the Memorial Hall, Farringdon Street, London, on February 27, 1900. Some seventy organisations were represented, the largest delegation coming from the Gas and General Workers' Union. The principal resolution on the agenda was a proposal "to establish a distinct Labour Group in Parliament who should have their own whips and agree upon their policy," and it was on this proposal that the battle was joined. First of all, was it desirable, or even possible, to form such a group, and, if formed, who should be allowed to join it and what was its policy to be? To begin with, not all the delegates present were convinced, in spite of the experience of the past twenty years, that an independent group in Parliament was necessary. Ramsay MacDonald, describing the Conference ten years later, wrote that some had come "to bury the attempt in good-humoured tolerance, a few to make sure that burial would be its fate but the majority determined to give it a chance."

The delegates who wanted a group established were divided into three sections—those who wished to see a Party formed composed exclusively of trade unionists; those who wanted to widen it to include men who sympathised with the aims of the Labour Movement, from whatever class they might spring (which at that juncture was for some one way of expressing a wish to work with the Liberals); and those who wanted to confine membership to avowed socialists whose beliefs were "based upon the recognition of the class war." This last view was held by the representatives of the Social Democratic Federation who pressed it with fervour. It stood no chance of acceptance however and was voted down by a combination of those who, though socialists, were neither Marxists nor convinced that the time was ripe to establish a purely socialist party; those who wanted a trade-union party only, and those who wanted no party at all.

The I.L.P. delegation was strongly in favour of independence on a non-socialist basis and it was this compromise between the two extremes which the Conference in the end accepted. It was decided "to establish a Labour Group with its own whips and policy" and further that such a group "should be ready to co-operate with any party which for the time being was engaged in promoting legislation in the interests of Labour but be equally ready to associate with any party opposing measures having the opposite tendency." This was a substantial victory for Hardie and MacDonald who believed that the one thing that mattered was to get an independent group formed. They scored an additional triumph when they got the delegates to agree not to countenance trade unionists and socialist candidates opposing each other at elections—an agreement not always honoured in the immediate years ahead.

James Keir Hardie, 1856-1915
Drawing by Cosmo Rowe

The only man present at the Conference with a national standing comparable to Hardie's was John Burns. Hardie had lost his seat in 1895 but Burns was still a Member of Parliament. He had been an early member of the Social Democratic Federation but those days were behind him. To him now its members were "factious, fanatical, intolerant, suspicious and ignorantly unpractical"; men who, like the Bourbons, neither learnt nor forgot. Bearded and heavy - browed, Burns's stocky figure in its perennial blue reefer suit was a familiar sight to Londoners, to whom his activities were always news. He supported the I.L.P. compromise but without enthusiasm. By this time his dislike of the S.D.F. point of view was beginning to extend to socialists generally and he had already begun to retreat from some of his earlier convictions. It was he who wittily said of socialists that "so anxious are they to reach the millennium that they sacrifice each other on the road." This calamity did not befall *him*. He ended his career as a Liberal Cabinet Minister. Events have proved that the acceptance of the I.L.P. compromise and the rejection of the doctrinaire proposals of the S.D.F. was right. Hardie and MacDonald were socialists; the I.L.P. was a socialist society; individual delegates from the trade unions were socialists, but by no means a majority of them, and, in any case, the unions they represented emphatically were not.

To set up the Labour Representation Committee—not until 1906 was its title changed to The Labour Party—was one thing: to make it succeed another. Membership was not open to individuals but only to Labour and socialist organisations who applied for affiliation and subscribed a small *per capita* fee. Active opposition to the project continued. By no means all trade unions joined. Some, notably the miners'—a powerful organisation even then, with a dozen or so M.P.s in the House (that is to say M.P.s elected and supported by money found by the Union)—held aloof. Nor was there agreement in the Committee itself on some of the pressing problems then before Parliament. That, in spite of these difficulties, the L.R.C. not only lived but thrived was due to Ramsay MacDonald, its first Secretary, at £25 a year, loyally supported by Frederick Rogers, its first Chairman. Rogers is now unfortunately remembered by few. Born in Whitechapel in 1846 he had begun life as an errand boy to an ironmonger at 2*s*. a week but later followed the craft of book-binding in vellum. Self-taught (the first Education Act was not passed until 1870) and greatly influenced by the writings of Charles Kingsley, F. D. Maurice, Ruskin and other Christian Socialists, he became an authority on Elizabethan literature, was a notable Shakespearean scholar and could talk learnedly on church architecture—English and European. In 1900 he was Organising Secretary of the Old Age Pensions Committee, a post he had been persuaded to take by the Rt. Hon. Charles Booth, author of *Life and Labour of the People of London*, and F. Herbert Stead, Warden of Browning Hall Settlement, Walworth.

Soon after the Labour Representation Committee had established itself in a room in Ramsay MacDonald's flat in Lincoln's Inn Fields it was faced with a General Election. Short though the time had been to prepare, fifteen candidates managed to take the field, among them Ramsay MacDonald, Philip Snowden, Keir Hardie, George Lansbury, Richard Bell, and Will Thorne. Only two of them were elected, however; Hardie was returned for Merthyr Tydfil, and Richard Bell, Secretary of the Amalgamated Society of Railway Servants, won Derby. John Burns also fought but not under the auspices of the Committee. Support for the Committee however grew steadily, taking a spectacular leap forward after the House of Lords had, in the Taff Vale case, declared the funds of the unions liable for breaches of contract and other offences committed by their members. This judgment read a new meaning into the legislation of 1871 and 1875 and caused consternation. By 1902 the affiliated membership of the Committee almost doubled, rising from 455,450 to 861,000. During the next two years also it won three by-elections. David Shackleton, who had started life as a half-timer in the mills, was returned unopposed for Clitheroe; Will Crooks, an East End workhouse cockney with more than his share of cockney wit, won Woolwich and Arthur Henderson carried Barnard Castle after a hard fight.

In 1903 the Annual Conference of the Committee took a momentous step, indicative both of its growing importance and the increased support it was getting from the unions. It decided that for the future its members in the House should "abstain strictly from identifying themselves with, or promoting the interests of, any section of the Liberal or Conservative

Parties"; that its endorsed candidates should "accept this pledge or resign"; and that they should "appear before their constituencies under the title of Labour Candidates only." The same Conference decided to levy its affiliated organisations for the purpose of maintaining its members in the House and to assist in meeting their election expenses. Contributions were fixed at one penny per member per year and no drawings were to be made on the Fund until a sum of £2,500 had been accumulated, when all M.P.s returned under the L.R.C. banner were to receive £200 per annum. There was no payment of Members in those days.

'MAY-DAY 1907'
Cartoon by Walter Crane

THE GROUP BECOMES A PARTY

THE Committee entered the General Election of 1906 better prepared for the struggle than it had been in 1900. It had tightened its rules and was now free of all entanglements with other Parties. It had increased the number of organisations affiliated to it from fifty-one to two hundred and thirty-three and its membership from 375,931 to nearly a million. It had taken steps to provide some financial assistance to its elected representatives, though at this period the funds available for all purposes were astonishingly small; and, most important of all, it had fifty candidates strategically placed in areas calculated to yield the maximum results.

The Election was a great triumph for the Liberal Party. After years in the wilderness it returned to power with a substantial majority, administering a crushing defeat to the Tories and to Joseph Chamberlain's policy of tariff reform. Tory Ministers had gone down like ninepins. Arthur Balfour, then Prime Minister, had been defeated: even Henry Chaplin, who had sat for Sleaford for goodness knows how long, had been dislodged—by a vegetarian who toured the constituency on a bicycle! When the final results were declared only one hundred and fifty-seven Tories had survived in a House of six hundred and seventy.

No less sensational was the success of the Labour Party, as it was henceforward to be called. Of the fifty candidates who had gone to the poll twenty-nine had been returned. Not only had Henderson, Shackleton, Crooks and Hardie, its four members in the old House, easily retained their seats but they were joined by MacDonald, Snowden, Clynes, Barnes, Thorne and others all destined to become outstanding Parliamentarians. The nation suddenly realised that a new and formidable political force had arisen. The Press was full of speculation on its portent.

In the new Parliament the Party not only achieved at least one direct success—in the passage of the Education (Provision of Meals) Act, which gave local authorities power to provide meals for necessitous schoolchildren—but also had considerable influence on the trend of legislation. This was due in part to the fact that the Liberal Government recognised it, small though it was, as a serious competitor for working class support and partly to the fact that the Liberals had within their own ranks a substantial trade union section they did not want to lose. In addition, urged forward by its own Radical wing, the Liberal Party was willing, indeed anxious, to carry through a number of long-needed reforms which could be fitted into the existing framework of society.

All this notwithstanding, the Labour Party was in an invidious situation. It most decidedly, and its supporters equally decidedly, wanted to see the Trades Disputes Bill, introduced by the Government to undo some of the mischief caused by the Taff Vale Judgment, become law and the only

'THE LABOUR MEMBER'
Cartoon by Sir Max Beerbohm

realistic way to assure this was to support the Liberals. Having played the leading role in the agitation for Old Age Pensions it was equally anxious to see the Measure providing these placed on the Statute Book. Other Bills to provide for Workmen's Compensation, an eight-hour day for miners, National Health Insurance and Trades' Boards for the sweated industries also had its approval. These were reforms it had long advocated. Such trailing along in the wake of the Liberals however, though reasonable and indeed necessary in the circumstances, caused misunderstanding among the rank and file outside, many of whom and particularly the socialists were waging a ceaseless war against that Party in the constituencies. To them Liberalism and Toryism were indistinguishable. Both were anti-Labour and anti-socialist. The I.L.P. men in the House were well aware of this feeling. After all it was their organisation which was doing the bulk of the proselytising in the country. "We are," said Hardie in 1912, "already overweighted by the Liberal alliance. We attract to our ranks the best of the active, rebellious spirits in the working class. They do not expect impossibilities but they cannot brook being always called upon to defend and explain away the actions of the Parliamentary Labour Party."

This sense of political frustration was deepened by growing unrest in industry. Prices were rising but wages remained static. Between 1900 and 1911 the wholesale price of foodstuffs rose by 11·6 per cent whilst the increase in wages amounted to only 0·31 per cent. In the cotton trade twenty-four per cent, and in the woollen and worsted trades over sixty per cent, of those employed earned under 15*s*. a week whilst thousands of railwaymen earned less than 20*s*. Even those princes among the workers, the iron and steel trades employees, earned no more than an average of 32*s*. a week when fully employed. Strikes therefore became frequent, the flame of revolt being fanned by those who repudiated Parliamentary democracy altogether, preaching that only by direct action could the workers obtain redress of their grievances.

The leading apostle of direct action, or syndicalism as it was called, was Tom Mann, who had imported his gospel from the Continent. Like so many more, Mann had been aroused by the propaganda of Henry George in the early eighteen-eighties and, like so many others, it had led him to expound not the Single Tax but something quite different. As an ardent trade unionist he had helped to organise the dockers' strike in 1889 and as an equally ardent socialist he had joined first the Social Democratic Federation and afterwards the I.L.P. He was Secretary of the latter body from 1895 to 1898 when, disappointed by the inertia of the masses, he had emigrated to Australia. He returned to England in 1910 and shortly afterwards visited Paris where he was impressed by the growth of syndicalism in the French unions. Thereafter, he devoted himself to the work of building up a similar movement in Great Britain. He taught that political differences were external; that only in the workshop could fundamental unity and identity of interest be found and, consequently, real solidarity achieved. The workers therefore, he said, by using their industrial power aright could overthrow the existing structure of society and replace it by one more nearly moulded to their hearts' desire. It is impossible to say what success syndicalism might have had in this country had war not broken out in 1914. It attracted some interest among the workers and gathered some recruits. It failed however to survive the struggle of 1914-18.

PHILIP SNOWDEN, 1864-1937
Cartoon by Matt, 1924

Two elections occurred in 1910 following the action of the House of Lords who, in defiance of constitutional practice, had thrown out the 1909 Finance Bill because it contained clauses providing for the taxation of land values. Here again the Labour Party was at a disadvantage. The struggle was clearly a fight between those who were for and those who were against the right of the non-elected Upper Chamber to override the will of the elected representatives and on this issue the Liberals were not unnaturally identified as the Party all good democrats should vote for. To vote Labour, it was said, was to run the risk of letting the Tory in, a tragedy to be avoided at all costs.

The twenty-nine Labour M.P.s who had been returned in 1906 had had their numbers increased by the adherence of the miners' Members following the affiliation of their Union to the Party. In addition, in 1907, a fiery young Manchester student named Victor Grayson had fought and won the Colne Valley division of the West Riding as a socialist in defiance both of the I.L.P. and the Labour Party. Party strength in the House was therefore forty-five and it is an indication that its successes in 1906 had been no flash in the pan that in spite of the commanding advantages enjoyed by the Liberals and the popularity of the appeal of People versus Peers, the Party emerged from the two 1910 elections with a net loss of only three seats.

It put up fifty-six candidates in the Election held in December 1910, twenty-two less than in the previous January. This decrease was due to the Osborne Judgment which had had a crippling effect on the political funds of the unions. Osborne, a foreman railway porter and a branch Secretary of the Amalgamated Society of Railway Servants, had objected strongly to part of his contributions to the Union being used to secure Parliamentary representation—and Labour Party representation at that—and he had backed up his objection by bringing an action against the Society and its Trustees. As a result the Law Lords had laid it down that a trade union was acting illegally in raising a compulsory levy on its members for political purposes. This decision made it almost impossible for the unions to promote candidatures and, if it had not been for the fact that payment of Members was introduced in 1911, many of their men would have had to withdraw from Parliament. In 1913 an Act was passed by the Liberal Government to permit trade unions to raise money from their members for political purposes provided it was kept in a separate fund and that no member who objected was obliged to contribute.

THE FIRST WORLD WAR

WAR came in August 1914 and profoundly changed the fortunes of both the Liberal and Labour Parties. At its advent the Liberal Party, though harried by the militant suffragettes, confronted by the threat of open rebellion in Ulster and faced with grave industrial unrest at home, was still dominant. At its close, that great Party was irretrievably split and Lloyd George, its most spectacular personality, was in league with its hereditary foes. Before war came, the Parliamentary Labour Party, whilst not losing ground, was certainly making no great headway. It was sectional in composition and had no clearly defined policy. Its authority in the unions was being undermined by the direct-actionists campaigning for workers' control and many of its socialist supporters openly derided it for its supposed impotence. At the armistice it emerged a national Party with a detailed programme making a wide appeal.

The Labour Movement both in and outside Parliament was divided on the war. The Trades Union Congress and a majority of Labour M.P.s supported it whilst the I.L.P. and five of its Members in the House, Ramsay MacDonald, Keir Hardie, F. W. Jowett, Tom Richardson and, upon his return from abroad, Philip Snowden, opposed it. This difference of view led immediately, first, to the issue by the T.U.C. and the Labour Party of a joint manifesto "to clear away, once and for all, misconceptions which had been circulated as to the attitude of the British Labour Movement to the conflict" and, second, to the resignation of Ramsay MacDonald from the leadership of the Parliamentary Party, a position he had assumed upon Hardie's retirement from that post in 1911.

The catastrophe to the world and the apparent wreck of all he had striven for was too much for Hardie. In August 1915, worn out and broken-hearted, he died. MacDonald, though he still attended the House and occasionally spoke, no longer took a leading part in its proceedings. He made one attempt to join an ambulance unit but was arrested by the Belgians and deported as an undesirable character. Thereafter whilst the storm lasted, vilified and abused, he devoted himself to writing for the *Labour Leader* and working for the I.L.P. This was a great change for him. Up to that moment his position had been unassailable. He stood next to Keir Hardie in the affections of their followers and second to none, Snowden not excepted, as a political writer and a speaker. By every test he was acceptable. He had a commanding and handsome presence and, though born with no material advantages and largely self-educated, was of considerable intellectual stature. He had known what it was like to exist in London as an ill-paid clerk at 12*s.* 6*d.* a week. He had at the age of twenty-two sent Hardie a message of good will when the latter raised the banner of revolt in Mid-Lanark and had himself fought a forlorn contest at Southampton in 1895 as Labour candidate. At the outbreak of war he had been a member of the I.L.P. for twenty years and could claim to have done more than any other individual at that time towards establishing the Labour Party itself.

ARTHUR HENDERSON, 1863-1935
Bust by K. S. de Strobl

In 1916 a Coalition Government was formed in which Arthur Henderson became President of the Board of Education with a seat in the Cabinet. Later in the same year further changes occurred. Lloyd George superseded Asquith as Prime Minister; John Hodge, a steel-smelter, became Minister of Labour, George Barnes Minister of Pensions and Henderson a member of the War Cabinet. Henderson however resigned from the Government in August 1917 following a difference with his Cabinet colleagues over the participation of the British Labour Movement in an international socialist conference it was proposed to hold in Stockholm. This conference had been initiated by Kerensky, following the first phase of the Russian Revolution, and Henderson, who had visited Russia on behalf of the British Government, was of the opinion that it was desirable that British Labour should be represented. In October Kerensky fell and the Bolsheviks came to power. Shortly afterwards Russia was out of the war.

Arthur Henderson was now free to return to his post as Secretary of the Party. Astute politician that he was, he saw clearly that the moment had come to broaden the basis of the Party by the admittance of individual members and to provide it with a policy—in short to transmute it into a national organisation with a national appeal. At that date the structure of the Party had altered little during the eighteen years of its existence. It was still, as it had been in 1900, a loose federation of trade unions, socialist societies, trades and labour councils and a few local election committees. Individuals, as individuals, could not become members. The most they could do was to join, if they were eligible, a branch of an affiliated trade union or of one of the affiliated socialist societies. In either case their prime loyalty was to their union or to their society and not to some shadowy Party in the background to which their organisation paid yearly dues. A new Representation of the People Act however was in the making which would enfranchise for the first time many millions, including at least six millions of women. It seemed to Henderson therefore essential that, if these voters were to be reached and increased representation obtained, electoral machinery must be established in the constituencies and local supporters harnessed direct to the work of building and maintaining it.

A NATIONAL PARTY

PROPOSALS to amend the constitution of the Party in order to admit individual members and to set up electoral machinery in the constituencies were put forward at the Annual Conference held in Nottingham, January 1918, when it was decided to convene a special gathering a month later to consider them. At this second Conference it was agreed to continue the existing system of direct affiliation by trade unions and other national organisations but to establish in addition Constituency Parties in each Parliamentary area. These Parties are to-day the focal point of all political propaganda work in the Divisions. Normally, they function through a small Executive Committee drawn from, and acting for, a larger General Committee which in turn is composed of representatives of the various units—Individual Members' and Women's Sections; Leagues of Youth; Trades Councils; Trade Union and Co-operative Society branches—in the towns, villages, wards and polling districts in

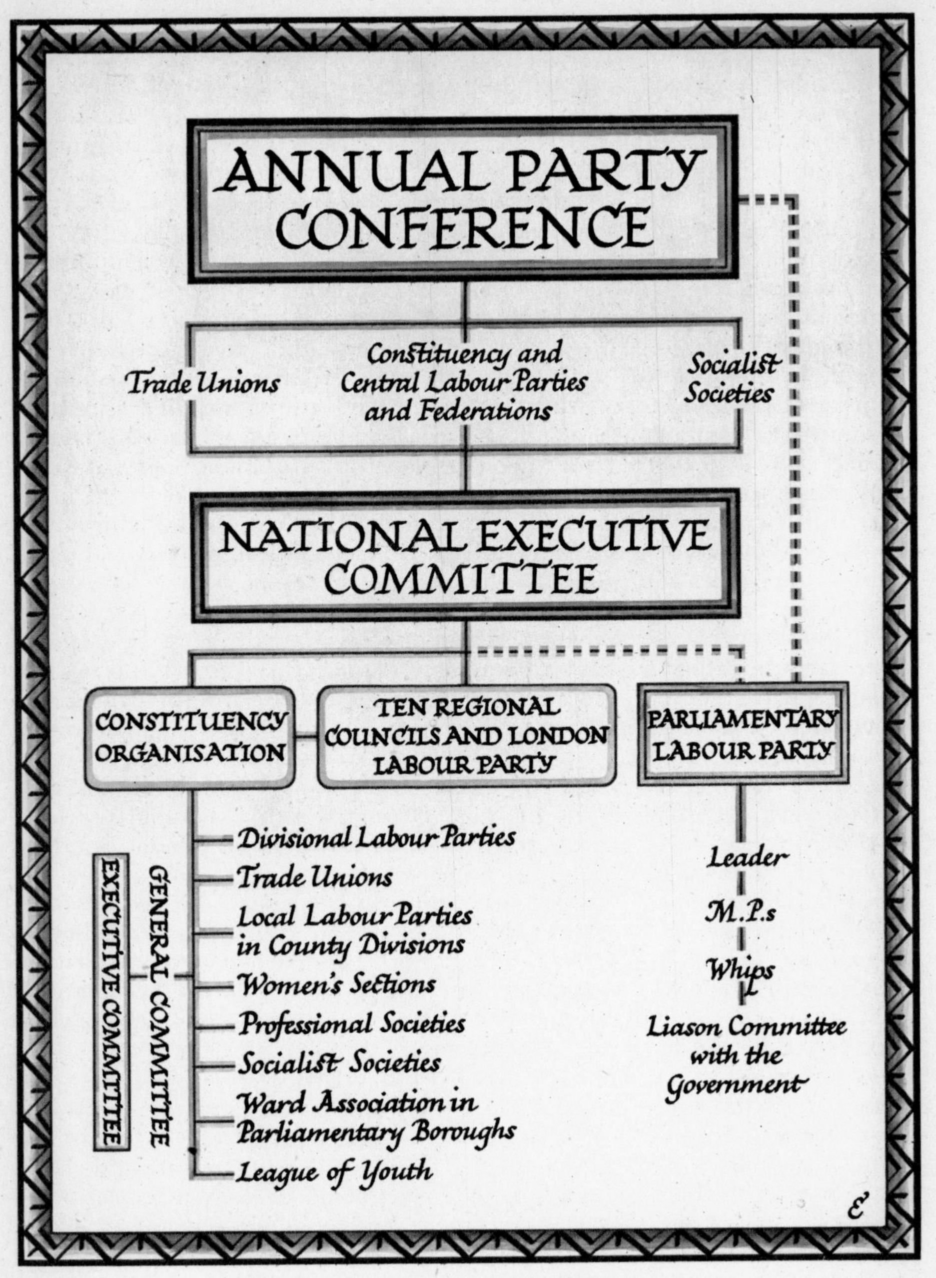

CHART OF THE LABOUR PARTY ORGANISATION

the area. It is the Constituency Party which appoints the agent, confirms the selection of individuals to fight local-authority elections, nominates the Parliamentary candidate, designates the delegates to Annual Conference and is the body with which Headquarters deals.

The affiliation fee to the National Party is now sixpence a member a year. National organisations remit this direct to the Party in London on the total of their political membership whilst Constituency Parties pay on the number of membership cards received from London and issued to local supporters. Although sixpence a member is the sum laid down, Constituencies are free to fix their subscription rates from their local members and local parties at their own figure. Most of them now fix a minimum of at least a penny a week but receive a good deal more than this from those able to afford it. Considerable sums are also raised in the course of the year from concerts, whist drives, bazaars, the sale of literature and collections at meetings. In all these activities the women members take a leading share and many a thriving Party with a substantial balance at the bank owes its solvency and its strength to the sacrificial work of its womenfolk. It is they who do most of the canvassing, they who spend long hours sewing and otherwise preparing for the annual Christmas Fair, and they who cut the bread and butter and wash up at the numerous social events held in the course of the year.

In addition to the sixpenny affiliation fee, Constituency Parties are under an obligation to subscribe to a National Insurance Fund which gives them the right to a substantial grant should they be involved in a by-election. The effect of this arrangement is that no Division, however backward and poor, need shirk a fight for lack of money and that all constituencies can concentrate their efforts on day-to-day propaganda and towards making provision for the next General Election without the fear that their funds may be depleted by an earlier contest. Under another scheme all Constituency Parties putting up a candidate at a General Election are expected to subscribe the sum of £5 to a special fund in return for which Headquarters guarantees to make good the Returning Officer's deposit of £150 should it be forfeited. Both these schemes have been in operation for over twenty years and both have proved an unqualified success.

The income of the National Party from all sources now approaches £200,000 a year, compared with just over £200 in the first year of its existence. Some of this money is received for particular purposes but the remainder is used over a wide and varied field. The Party not only has large offices and a large staff in London but ten regional offices in various parts of the country to which men and women organisers are attached. At Transport House, in addition to departments dealing with the substantial volume of day-to-day organisation, secretarial and accounting work, it has sections specialising in research, international questions, publicity in all its forms, including the preparation and issue of leaflets, pamphlets,

POSTER PUBLISHED BY THE LABOUR PARTY, 1929

Coloured lithograph by G. Spencer Pryse

posters and periodicals. It also, in association with the T.U.C., maintains an up-to-date reference library. Among its activities it runs correspondence courses in organisation, method, and electoral law, holds examinations to test the proficiency of those taking them and awards certificates. Most of those who thus qualify become Party agents, Constituencies being encouraged to employ them. Those Constituencies that do are helped with grants towards their agent's salary on a diminishing scale over a period of years.

The supreme authority in the Party is the Annual Conference, to which all affiliated organisations are entitled to submit resolutions and to send delegates. It is Conference that makes policy and to which the Parliamentary Party and the National Executive Committee report on the happenings of the previous twelve months.

The National Executive Committee however stands in a closer relationship to Annual Conference than does the Parliamentary Party. The National Executive is directly elected by Conference itself, meets regularly throughout the year, and is the body upon which falls the duty of interpreting, and implementing, its decisions. Labour Members of Parliament, on the other hand, though of course members of the Party, are elected by, and owe their first allegiance to, their constituents. They attend Conference therefore only in an *ex officio* capacity, and are allowed to take part in the discussions but are not allowed to vote unless they are also there as delegates from an affiliated organisation. The Leader of the Party is always an *ex officio* member both of Conference and of the National Executive Committee. He is however elected not by Conference but by the Parliamentary Party.

The Conference which set up Constituency Parties, and by so doing made possible the organisation just described, also enlarged the objects for which the Party stood. For the first time, it was laid down that the aim of the Party was the establishment of a socialist commonwealth in which "the workers by hand and by brain" would "secure the full fruits of their industry," a declaration which, in view of the Party's subsequent achievement of power, must be reckoned a major event in British political history. Earlier in the same year Conference had adopted a statement of Allied War Aims, prepared by Henderson, MacDonald and Sidney Webb, which outlined a framework upon which a lasting peace could be built and, anticipating coming events, suggested the establishment of a "League of Nations which not only all the present belligerents but every other independent State should be pressed to join." During 1918 the Party also adopted and issued its first detailed programme under the title of *Labour and the New Social Order*. This document, the work of Sidney Webb, who represented the Fabian Society on the National Executive, sold in large numbers and aroused considerable interest. Arnold Bennett characterised it as a publication "of first-rate social importance which everybody

'SIDNEY WEBB ON HIS BIRTHDAY, 1919'
Cartoon by Sir Max Beerbohm

could afford to buy, which everybody ought to read, and which everybody of average intelligence could read with pleasure."

As the War neared its close it became evident that the Coalition would not end as expected when the fighting stopped but that the Prime Minister and those associated with him would try to extend its life by appealing as a Government to the country for a new mandate. Few however imagined that the appeal would be made as soon as it was. Almost before the signatures were dry on the terms of surrender a General Election was announced. Under the leadership of Lloyd George the administration sought a renewal of confidence which, intoxicated with victory, the electors proceeded to give in no uncertain fashion. Lloyd George candidates were returned in great numbers. Those who had opposed the War, like MacDonald and Snowden, and those who had only opposed a continuance of the Coalition, like Henderson, were heavily defeated. The Labour Party put up three hundred and sixty-one candidates (of which fifty-seven were successful) and polled 2,244,945 votes. This was its first trial of strength as a national Party and considering the atmosphere of patriotic bitterness in which the contest was fought it was numerically not a bad result, though it was regrettable that most of its Parliamentary leaders had gone down in the struggle. The Liberal Party, brilliantly represented by an outstanding team in the old House, suffered a severe setback.

The new Government soon ran into trouble. Overwhelmingly composed of Conservatives impatient of controls and anxious to return to normal, its policy vacillated in the face of developing industrial unrest and disgruntled soldiers needing houses. A nation-wide strike occurred on the railways; the engineers were locked out; strife broke out in the mines. As the years passed the cost of living went down and with it wages—even more rapidly. Unemployment mounted. It was obvious that the popularity of the Government was fading, a fact the Tories in it did not fail to note. Nor did they fail to observe that support for the Labour Party was increasing. The Party had won a number of by-elections and had registered considerable gains in the municipal elections, particularly in London. They were also aware that the life of Parliament was running out and that soon, within twelve months at the most, an Election must be held.

In October 1922, the dissidents among the Tories, led by Stanley Baldwin, broke up the Coalition, their hope being that if they forced an Election then and went to the country under their own banner they would escape the wrath that must inevitably fall on the outgoing Administration. Their hope was justified. The electors found no difficulty in sorting the Tory lambs from the Lloyd George goats and in spite of the fact that, as the dominant partners in the old Government, they were primarily responsible for the mess, the Tories achieved a substantial triumph. Labour however likewise registered gains. It numbered one hundred and forty-two in the new House and became, for the first time, His Majesty's Official Opposition. It was this Parliament which saw the advent of the Clydeside contingent, among them James Maxton, to Westminster and the return of Ramsay MacDonald both to the House and to the Leadership. Maxton, with his lean head, long lank black hair and deep-set eyes under bushy brows, looked as fierce as the proverbial pirate king but, endowed with a melodious voice and a sweet sense of phrasing, no one was more able than he to make a revolutionary utterance sound like a lover's caress.

THE TRANQUIL TWENTIES

THE 1922 Parliament was short-lived. Notwithstanding the supposedly stimulating effect of safe Tory rule on industry, the country did not prosper. Suddenly, in the autumn of 1923, Stanley Baldwin, who had succeeded Bonar Law as Prime Minister, seeking a way out of the nation's troubles, decided to appeal to the people on a Protectionist policy. This was of course an issue upon which all true Liberals could rally. The followers of Asquith and the adherents of Lloyd George accordingly temporarily patched up their differences and in consequence greatly increased their strength in the House. One hundred and fifty-eight Liberals were returned to two hundred and fifty-eight Tories. Labour won one hundred and ninety-one seats—fifty more than the year before. It was making headway. The Tories were still the largest Party in the House but they could only carry on if the Liberals supported them. Asquith thus held the balance and speculation was rife as to what he would do. In the end, the Liberals combined with Labour to defeat the Government on the Address and the King sent for Ramsay MacDonald.

There were those, wise after the event, who declared that Labour should have refused to accept office without power. Be this as it may, it has to be recorded that with the support of the Liberals, grudgingly given and equally grudgingly accepted, the first Labour Government staggered from crisis to crisis through eleven depressing months until, in the autumn of 1924, it was thrown out by the two older Parties acting together, who alleged that political pressure had been responsible for the dropping of the prosecution of the editor of a Communist newspaper.

The 1923-24 Parliament was however not entirely barren of achievement. Though its minority position prevented it from instituting any far-reaching reforms, the Labour Party did, with Liberal help, increase the allowances, and improve the conditions, of the unemployed, the old-age pensioners and the war-disabled, and passed the Wheatley Housing Act designed to build two and a half million houses in fifteen years. In foreign affairs, it resumed diplomatic relations with Russia and negotiated trade treaties with her. It took the lead in calling the London Conference, which approved a scheme for settling outstanding problems connected with the payment of reparations by Germany, and was responsible for the Geneva Protocol—considered and agreed to by the League Assembly that year but not afterwards ratified by the succeeding Government.

The General Election that followed, the third in two years, is notable for the use made by the Party's opponents of the notorious Zinoviev Letter. This document, now believed to have been a forgery, urged that Communist propaganda should be increased among British sailors and soldiers in order to hasten the overthrow of the capitalist system. The Labour Party was of course violently opposed both to Communism and to the use of force as a political weapon, but the fact that it had recognised the Russian Government and was anxious to make a trade treaty with it as part of the work of pacification in Europe was enough. From then on the Bolshevik bogey played an increasing role in the conflict and materially helped Stanley Baldwin to return to power with a solid majority of two hundred and twenty-two over all other Parties combined. The Labour Party increased its poll by over a million but lost forty seats.

From the Party point of view the period of the second Baldwin administration was noteworthy for the issue of *Labour and the Nation*, a

A South Wales Mining Village
Drawing by Adolf Dehn, 1926

detailed re-statement of Labour policy, the first draft of which was prepared by R. H. Tawney, and for the General Strike which began on May 4, 1926, and lasted nine days.

This struggle, in which the whole Labour Movement, industrial and political, took part, was the culmination of a dispute between the mine-owners and the miners which had begun in July 1925 when the owners, in order to terminate the then existing national agreement and to revert to the eight-hour day, had issued lock-out notices to the men. Two things were at that juncture clear: one that if the lock-out took effect the transport and railway workers would support the miners by refusing to handle coal, and, two, that the reserves of coal were too small to enable the Government to face a prolonged stoppage with equanimity. The Prime Minister was in a dilemma. He had committed himself to the assertion that all the workers of the country had got to take reductions of wages, which meant that he sympathised with the owners in their desire to reduce costs by lengthening hours. He had also declared more than once that no subsidy would be given to the coal industry which meant, if he persisted in that view, that a clash, for which the Government was ill-prepared, was inevitable. Astute politician that he was, he decided to go back on what he had said and to grant a subsidy. This was however to be for a period of nine months only whilst a Royal Commission to be set up was holding an enquiry. The lock-out notices were accordingly withdrawn, and the

Commission commenced to sit. Meanwhile as a precaution coal stocks were quietly built up.

The Report of the Commission was published in March 1926 and satisfied neither side. It said that a drastic reorganisation of the industry was necessary, which annoyed the owners, and recommended readjustments of wage-rates and conditions, which annoyed the men. Wages in the industry were shockingly low, the *average* being 10*s*. 7¾*d*. for a seven-hour shift—which took no account of the time actually spent underground, working places often being a mile or two from the shaft bottom. On April 16 the owners once more posted lock-out notices, the Government remained passive, and on May 1, despite every effort by the T.U.C. to avert the catastrophe, the miners were out. Three days later they were joined by their fellow trade unionists from one end of the country to the other.

The solidarity with which all sections reacted to the call surprised the Government. Docks, railways, factories were deserted: newspapers ceased to appear, buses to run. Work went forward on housing schemes, and essential services like the distribution of food continued, otherwise the stoppage was complete. Stanley Baldwin, so it was reported, looked gloomy, Winston Churchill cheerful and energetic. The latter threw himself into the production of the *British Gazette*, a daily broadsheet designed to keep the country informed of the Government's case. The publication of the *British Gazette* led the General Council of the T.U.C. to issue a similar sheet, the *British Worker*, in support of the strikers. This was produced on the presses of the *Daily Herald* which had itself begun as a strike sheet in 1912.

The struggle was carried on in great good humour. There was little discord, practically no rioting; police and strikers were on the easiest of terms, often in fact playing football together. Foreign observers found it all very strange. It was obvious that the workers had come out in no revolutionary spirit but with the single aim of helping the miners at considerable sacrifice to themselves and to the funds of their unions. All the same, it was plain that no democratically elected Government, however badly it had handled the matter, could abrogate its authority in the face of such a threat. Very soon intermediaries were busy searching for a solution acceptable to both sides.

The agreement which brought the strike to an end was negotiated by Sir Herbert Samuel (afterwards Lord Samuel) who had been Chairman of the Royal Commission. Accepted by the T.U.C. and by the Government but rejected by the miners' leaders, this provided (*a*) for the setting-up of a National Wages Board under an independent chairman, (*b*) that there should be no revision of previous wage-rates unless sufficient assurances were forthcoming for a drastic reorganisation of the pits, and (*c*) that in any case reasonable rates should be fixed, below which no class of labour should in any circumstances be reduced. The miners remained out for nearly seven months after the General Strike had ended, and were driven back to work at last by sheer starvation. The eight-hour day was reimposed and wages reduced to an average of 9*s*. 3½*d*. a shift for a much higher output a man. So long as the miners continued the fight the Movement did all it could to help them financially but, unfortunately, nearly all the other unions had also dissipated their reserves in the struggle and were now themselves engaged in a losing battle against the employers, a majority of whom were in vindictive mood. The unions were further crippled by the passage of the Trades Disputes and Trades Union Act in 1927.

MARGARET BONDFIELD, THE FIRST WOMAN CABINET MINISTER, 1929-1931
Cartoon by Sallon

The failure of the General Strike, with its aftermath of bitterness and heavy debt for so many, did not have the unfavourable effect on the Party's election prospects confidently predicted by some. On the contrary, at the General Election of 1929 the electors rallied to its support in larger numbers than ever before. It won two hundred and eighty-seven seats, nearly thirty more than the Tories, and was for the first time the largest Party in the House. It was however still a minority of the Commons. Once again the Liberals with fifty-nine members held the balance.

The second Labour Government began well. Arthur Henderson particularly, as Foreign Secretary, did excellent work. He gave wholehearted support to the League, began slowly to come to terms with the democratic rulers of Germany and prepared the ground for a Disarmament Conference which it was proposed should be held in 1932.

Elsewhere however States were moving to disaster. The United States was drifting towards economic collapse. Unemployment there rose to staggering dimensions and banks began to close their doors. These events had their repercussions in Europe and in this country. By 1931, unemployment in Great Britain had risen to 21 per cent. The Budget was unbalanced —then reckoned a catastrophe of the first magnitude by the orthodox. At the insistence of the Liberals an Economy Committee was set up with Sir George May as Chairman. It reported that by 1932 the national deficit would reach £120,000,000. This total included the customary allocation of £50,000,000 to the Sinking Fund and the refund of £40,000,000 advanced to the Unemployment Insurance Fund—neither of which transfers were essential in the abnormal circumstances then prevailing. The Cabinet was divided on remedies. A majority was ready for economies but refused to agree to the inclusion among them of a substantial cut in unemployment benefits, and on this issue the Government split and fell. Ramsay MacDonald, Philip Snowden and J. H. Thomas, in association with the Tories and Liberals, formed a National Administration. The rest of the Labour Ministers, and all but a handful of Labour Members, went into opposition under the leadership of Arthur Henderson.

An Election followed, the bitterest in living memory, Snowden in particular turning venomously on his old colleagues. From a thousand platforms and over the B.B.C. the reckless extravagance of the Labour Government was blamed for what had occurred though nobody stopped to explain why, if this were true, MacDonald and Snowden, the men most responsible for so disastrous a financial policy, were retained and exalted. The Party suffered a crushing defeat, sinking from two hundred and ninety Members in the House to fifty-two.

THE UNEASY THIRTIES

THOUGH battered and bruised, the Party was not broken. Its electoral machinery remained intact. Not a single Constituency Party ratted. Slowly and painfully, licking their wounds, active supporters everywhere began to rebuild. In this work they received considerable, though involuntary, assistance from their opponents.

The National Government was an assorted bunch. Apart from a resolve to institute drastic economies in expenditure and to increase taxation, there was little in common between its various groups. This had been apparent at the Election when, individually, they had preached their own Party beliefs and, collectively, asked for a "doctor's mandate." Doctors' prescriptions are difficult for the layman to decipher, though normally doctors themselves know what they mean. Here, the doctors themselves fell out when it came to interpretation. Philip Snowden was the first to depart, complaining loudly of broken faith because the Tories repealed the Land Values clauses of his last Finance Act. The sacred ark of Free Trade was further mauled and, next, muttering sorrowfully that this had certainly not been part of the prescription, the Liberals likewise left.

As the months went by the international situation deteriorated. The Disarmament Conference, presided over by Arthur Henderson, petered out and with it went the last big chance to push back the looming menace of Nazism and to re-establish German democratic statesmen in the eyes of their disgruntled countrymen. Henderson, at this time sick and shortly to die, was a man of great integrity of spirit and of high resolve. Without the personal glamour of MacDonald, the cutting incisiveness of Snowden or the emotional approach of Lansbury, he could nevertheless sway a meeting, particularly a Party Conference, to a greater degree than any of them. Like many other Labour leaders of his generation, he was the product of the

By courtesy of the Artist

MR. ERNEST BEVIN AT THE UNO CONFERENCE, 1946
Detail from an oil painting by Feliks Topolski

Nonconformist Sunday School and was, to the end, a lay-preacher of his church. He had been Secretary of the Party since 1911, and had, with MacDonald, been intimately associated with its shaping. The Labour Movement remembers him both for his work for peace (for which he received the Nobel Prize in 1934) and for the Party organisation he built, which not even the storms of 1931 could breach. He was succeeded in the Secretaryship by James Middleton, who had been its Assistant Secretary for many years and a member of its staff almost since its birth. In the very early days he had been MacDonald's single helper when its only office was a room in MacDonald's flat in Lincoln's Inn Fields. His knowledge of the Movement, its personalities and its aims, was unequalled and at that juncture in the Party's history its organisation could not have been in better hands. His first wife, Mary Middleton, had been Mrs. MacDonald's closest friend and they had shared the work of the Women's Labour League in the early days. It was Mary Middleton's death in 1911, following as it did closely on the death of their own small boy David, which hastened Mrs. MacDonald's end. "The will to live," says Ramsay MacDonald in the moving *Memoir* he afterwards wrote, "seemed to go out of my wife . . . she told us that had she to begin life again, she would pray to be allowed to live it in the same way: she commended to us the people and the causes that she had been helping and on 8th September died when the sun was robing itself in its setting glory and filling the room with the mournful light of early evening."

The flat in Lincoln's Inn Fields was not only the office of the Party but also, until Mrs. MacDonald's death, its social centre. In the early nineteen-twenties Mrs. Sidney Webb, in an endeavour to provide a meeting-ground, at any rate for the wives of members, formed the Half Circle Club. Later the National Labour Club was established but had eventually to close down when it was found impossible to maintain it on a subscription sufficiently modest to allow the greatest number to join.

During 1935, the European scene grew darker. Hitler had enjoyed ruthless power for over two years and was rearming in defiance of the Treaty of Versailles. Mussolini was about to attack Abyssinia and it was proposed that the League should restrain him by the application of economic sanctions. Action of this kind might lead to war—an outcome George Lansbury, now Leader, could not as a pacifist contemplate. The Party however had never taken up the extreme pacifist position. It had always pinned its faith to Collective Security and wholehearted support of the League. It reaffirmed this policy at the Annual Conference in October and Lansbury resigned the Leadership. Lansbury's departure, together with the reason for his going, caused a flurry in the ranks. He had given his life to the service of mankind and was greatly beloved. Supporters had yet to be convinced by the march of events that a strong hand with dictators was necessary. To them, as to most ordinary folk, war was silly and

ELLEN WILKINSON, 1891-1947
Cartoon by Sallon

the thought of it at any time distressing. Members therefore were worried and perplexed. At this juncture, although Parliament had another year to run, Baldwin decided to appeal to the country.

The Party entered the Election under the stress of this change, as yet not entirely clear about the issues involved, but otherwise in good shape. It knew from the evidence it had from the constituencies that it would retrieve some at least of the ground lost in 1931. For one thing, it had been greatly enheartened by successes in local elections, the crowning triumph of which had been the capture of the London County Council the previous year. The astonishing hold which the Party has achieved in the Metropolitan area, locally and nationally, has of course been due to the self-sacrificing devotion of many stalwarts. Their efforts however would have been far less fruitful than they have been if it had not been for the organising genius of Herbert Morrison. As Secretary of the London Labour Party it was his hand that guided and advised the enthusiastic but raw men and women who began to find themselves in control of East End borough after borough in the nineteen-twenties: it was he, with them, who established highly efficient electoral machinery and worked out an acceptable and co-ordinated policy. His leadership of the Party on the L.C.C. has given London an imaginative and constructive administration which the voters by their continued support appear to value. In the 1945 General Election forty-eight out of sixty-two London divisions returned Labour Members.

As expected, the Party made substantial gains in the 1935 Election. Quietly but adroitly led by Clement Attlee, who had stepped temporarily into Lansbury's place, it more than trebled its membership. When the new House met, Attlee was confirmed in the leadership; Arthur Greenwood was elected deputy-Leader.

Unemployment during these years was widespread, particularly in what had become known as the depressed areas. On the Clyde, in South Wales and in the towns on the north-east coast there were thousands of young men in their twenties who had not only not done a day's work in their lives but saw no hope of getting one however long they lived. Public attention was focused on the tragedies being enacted in these areas by the decision of some of them to bring their plight to the direct notice of the Government by marching deputations to London to present their case.

The most spectacular perhaps of these was the contingent led by Ellen Wilkinson that marched the three hundred miles from Jarrow to London in twenty-five days. In Jarrow, in 1936, only one hundred men were employed in the iron, steel and shipbuilding industries where formerly eight thousand had worked. Thirteen local industries and dozens of shops had closed down.

Ellen Wilkinson was the product of a working-class home. She had passed from the elementary school by means of scholarships to Manchester University, where she took her M.A. degree in history and economics. From the University she went headlong into trade unionism, served for a time on the Manchester City Council and first entered Parliament in 1924 as M.P. for Middlesbrough East. Small in stature, with a great mop of red hair, she was recognised instantly wherever she went, and she went everywhere, for her vivid personality and brilliant and witty gifts as orator made her a much sought-after speaker. At the time of her death in February 1947 she was Minister of Education, the second woman to become a member of a British Cabinet.

Meanwhile, Mussolini had fallen upon the Ethiopians and less than twelve months later civil war broke out in Spain. Hitler marched unchecked into the Ruhr and shortly subjugated Austria to Nazi rule by an exhibition of thuggery till then unparalleled among civilised peoples. In September 1938, Sudetenland was handed by the British and French to Hitler who assured them that this was positively his "last territorial claim in Europe," but six months later he had absorbed Czechoslovakia. Tragically enough these

"You Know You Can Trust Us"
Election cartoon by Vicky, 1945

same years saw in this country a great rallying to the League. A Peace Ballot was organised. In spite of these efforts however the League sank and presently ceased to count—not because ordinary people had ceased to believe in it but because democratic statesmen no longer used it.

The shortcomings of the Government, in particular its policy of non-intervention in the Spanish Civil War, led to the organisation of a campaign to unite all parties of the Left. This agitation was carried on jointly by the Socialist League, the I.L.P. (now outside the Labour Party and but a fraction of its former self) and the Communist Party. Their main objective was to force the Government to lift its embargo on the supply of arms to the Spanish workers. The Socialist League was also involved in a similar campaign to establish a Popular Front in which it was hoped to unite Labour, Liberals and Communists for the purpose of ensuring the defeat of the Chamberlain Administration when the Election came. The Labour Party held aloof from these campaigns, re-affirming its refusal to enter into any agreement with the Communists. The Socialist League could not of course foresee what was to happen but the future was to demonstrate that the attitude adopted by the Party was the correct one. A linking-up with the Communists would have been a disaster for the Labour Party and would have greatly weakened the national effort when war broke out. For, by then, Germany and Russia had concluded a pact of non-aggression and this materially altered the attitude of British Communists to the conflict.

When war came in 1939 it was suggested that a national administration should be formed under Neville Chamberlain but the Labour Party had too deep a distrust of the policies he had followed to welcome it and the proposal was dropped. The suggestion was renewed in May 1940, following a critical debate on the Norwegian campaign which the Party turned into a vote of censure on the general conduct of the War. The Party was still unalterably opposed to entering any Ministry of which Chamberlain was the head, but intimated that it would be willing to enter such an Administration under the leadership of Winston Churchill. It was therefore the Labour Party and not the Tories that gave Churchill his great chance. In the new Government Clement Attlee became Lord Privy Seal and Deputy Prime Minister, Arthur Greenwood Minister without Portfolio, Ernest Bevin Minister of Labour and National Service, Herbert Morrison Minister of Supply, A. V. Alexander First Lord of the Admiralty, Hugh Dalton Minister of Economic Warfare and Sir William (afterwards Viscount) Jowitt Solicitor-General. Later, Sir Stafford Cripps joined the Ministry. It was Arthur Greenwood who, as Minister without Portfolio, invited Sir William Beveridge to examine and report upon the desirability of a comprehensive scheme of National Insurance. This Report became world-famous and was later translated into legislation by the Labour Government that came to power following the General Election of 1945.

ERNEST BEVIN
Bust by Jacob Epstein, 1943

OFFICE WITH POWER

THE overwhelming defeat of the Tories in the General Election of 1945 surprised everybody, including Winston Churchill himself who had believed, not unnaturally perhaps, that his popularity and tremendous prestige would carry his Party to victory. The Labour Party won three hundred and ninety-three seats—one hundred and forty-seven over all other parties and groups together. Seventy-nine constituencies returned a Labour Member for the first time, many of them rural areas previously reckoned Tory strongholds. Thirty-one members of the Conservative Government lost their seats, among them five Cabinet Ministers and eight others of Cabinet rank. The Liberal Party sank from eighteen to twelve, two hundred and ninety-five of their candidates being defeated. Twenty-four women were elected—twenty-two of them supporters of the Labour Party. The total votes cast for Labour candidates were 11,992,292: for the Tories 8,665,566: and for the Liberals 2,239,668. According to *The Times* the total votes cast for candidates supporting a Conservative Government were 9,960,809: for candidates against such a Government 15,012,489.

Winston Churchill was not at his best during the campaign. His handling of the issues was in striking contrast to that of his chief Liberal and Labour opponents. He broadcast four times and was injudicious enough to assert among other extravagances that no socialist system could be established without a political police and that a Labour Government, to carry out its policy, "would have to fall back upon some form of Gestapo." Whether he actually believed this nonsense is not certain but events were to prove, as Clement Attlee said in one of his very effective replies, that Mr. Churchill "underestimated the intelligence of the public."

The Party fought the Election on a programme which had a very wide circulation both at home and among the troops overseas as a pamphlet entitled *Let us Face the Future*—a straightforward statement of what a Labour Government hoped to accomplish within the lifetime of a single Parliament if given power. Stating that "the Labour Party makes no baseless promises" and that "the future will not be easy" it went on to outline a plan which could harness the spirit shown during the War and apply it to the tasks of peace. It proposed that the Bank of England should pass under public control and that certain selected industries and services—coal, transport, gas, electricity, and iron and steel—should be socialised in the interests of the community. It further proposed to expand and improve agriculture; to build houses to let; enlarge and improve educational facilities; and to implement the scheme, promised by all Parties, of full social insurance. It gave "clear notice" that, in carrying through this programme, it "would not tolerate obstruction of the people's will by the House of Lords." On the wider front, it pledged the Party in support of a new United Nations Organisation and of the advancement of India to responsible self-government; to the development of the Colonial dependencies in the interests of those living in them; and to co-operation with the other Dominions of the British Commonwealth. This was a bold programme involving fundamental changes in both the social and the economic structures of the nation not easy to undertake under the most favourable conditions, much less to carry through amid the unprecedented chaos and disorganisation resulting from the War.

CONCLUSION

In 1950 the Party will celebrate the jubilee of its foundation. It can then look back along the road it has come and take stock of the distance travelled since that February day in 1900 when it came into existence. Its paying membership has grown from under 376,000 to over 5,000,000 and its income from less than £300 a year to something approaching £200,000. When it began, its electoral machinery in the constituencies was negligible: to-day it has active Parties in almost every area. In its first Election it polled

62,698 votes: in 1945, 11,992,292. During the first six years of its existence its representatives in the House were never more than four and those drawn from the ranks of the organised workers. Though still closely allied with the trade unions, it now numbers its supporters among all sections of the community and attracts its representatives from all classes of society. Of the three hundred and ninety-three Labour Members elected to Parliament in 1945, one hundred and nineteen were nominees of the unions, whilst a substantial proportion of the rest came from the professions—law, journalism, accountancy, medicine, engineering, teaching: sixty-eight came from the fighting services. In March 1948, Labour controlled over three hundred local authorities, including sixteen county councils.

These successes have not been easily achieved. On the contrary, they have been slowly and painfully acquired through fifty years of constant effort in which the traditional soap-box played a big part and the art of persuasion was brought by long practice to a high pitch of excellence. "The Labour Party," said Lord Oxford and Asquith speaking to Liberal Members of Parliament in 1924, "furnish us with a much needed lesson and example. No one who has not seen it at work and come into personal contact with the results can realise with what thoroughness and, I will add, with what practical sagacity its propaganda is carried on."

'TO BE OR NOT TO BE'
SIR STAFFORD CRIPPS
Drawing by Vicky, 1948

The test of success however is not the achievement of power, necessary though that is as a first step, but the use made of that power when won. It is a source of considerable satisfaction to supporters that, in less than four years from the date it assumed office, the Labour Government implemented the major part of the programme put before the electors in 1945. The more thoughtful among them however realise that a new social order cannot be created by legislation alone, much less built within the lifetime of a single Parliament. They see clearly that if the old sanctions of unemployment and poverty, which force individuals to work under a capitalist system of society, are to be discarded others, freely accepted, will have to take their place. A new outlook will have to be cultivated in which effort for the commonweal, to the end that all may be served, must be the guiding motive.

Pessimists will assert that, human nature being what it is, the British people are incapable of sufficient self-discipline to make this possible. They may be right but the supporters of the Labour Party do not share their view. On the contrary, they believe that as the community advances to higher social and economic standards it will also rise to a fuller realisation of its responsibilities. They agree in fact with Disraeli that "increased means and increased leisure are the two civilisers of man."

DR. EDITH SUMMERSKILL
Drawing by Feliks Topolski

SHORT BIBLIOGRAPHY

Short History of the British Working-Class Movement 1789-1937 by G. D. H. Cole. 1937, Allen & Unwin.—*A History of Factory Legislation* by B. L. Hutchins and A. Harrison. 1926, P. S. King & Son.—*A History of British Socialism* by Max Beer. 1940, Allen & Unwin.—*The History of Trade Unionism* by Sidney and Beatrice Webb. 1926, Longmans.—*Fabian Essays*, ed. G. Bernard Shaw. 1889, London.—*Practical Socialism for Britain* by Hugh Dalton. 1935, Routledge.—*The Case for Socialism* by Fred Henderson (new edition). 1933, Labour Party, London.—*The Life and Struggles of W. Lovett* by William Lovett. 1876, London.—*James Ramsay MacDonald, Labour's Man of Destiny* by H. Hessell Tiltman. 1929, Jarrolds.—*Arthur Henderson, a biography* by Mary Agnes Hamilton. 1938, Heinemann.—*Mr. Attlee* by Roy Jenkins. 1948, Heinemann